Diamond in the Rough:
Inspirations of Truth, Tragedy and Triumph

Published By:
RDW Creations, L.L.C.
Detroit, MI.
www.rdwcreations.com

isbn-10:   0615600883
isbn-13:   978-0615600888

Cover Design By:
A-Team Designs
www.a-teamdesigns.com

Diamond: From the ancient Greek word adámas - "unbreakable"

A Huge Heart-Felt Thanks!!

A-Team Designs

CheriTree Productions

Sylvia Hubbard &

Motown Writers Network

This book is dedicated in memory of my mother

Betty Ann White.

Contents

Preface

What began as a simple pleasure has now evolved into my life's passion. Writing is no longer just a leisure activity- it is a necessity of my being! I aspire to write with the purpose of uplifting others because everyone could use some inspiration nowadays. No matter whom you are, or what your circumstances may be, all of us have need for enthusiasm! Facebook, My Space, and Twitter are all modern modes of social media. People use these online tools to connect with others, vent frustrations, and share their opinions with the world. The idea is to spread a message to the masses. Although today this is the most popular form of communication, it is not the only era in which a social movement influenced a generation. Historically, written forms of communications have always had influential purposes and lasting effects.

The mind is both complex and deceptive. Sometimes our emotions can cloud our judgment. Putting words on paper not only creates clarity, but it also allows the reader to discover (or rediscover) what is hidden. The Harlem Renaissance era is the greatest literary movement in African American history. During the 1920s and 1930s, black writers and artist contributed their literary gifts in an effort to engage the black community. Writers were eager to express their frustrations, draw attention to the seriousness of social issues, as well as provide hope to their people. Following the American Civil War in 1865, racism was strong and economic opportunities few. Blacks continued to suffer extreme hardships prompting the need for creative self-expression.

This African American literary movement brought about an opportunity for writers to freely express their sensitivities about cultural differences. As director of the National Urban League, Charles S. Johnson was instrumental in supporting young black artists and authors who contributed during the Harlem Renaissance era. W.E.B. Dubois was able to bring attention to racial injustices of black people while editing the NAACP's journal <u>The Crisis</u>. Zora Neale Hurston devoted her works to this movement by focusing on the struggles within the black culture, and her personal trial toward success. These authors along with many others, helped pave the way for group expression (a.k.a social media). It is through their commitment they conveyed messages of frustration, hope and courage.

The Harlem Renaissance earned its' name in part, to the massive number of blacks that migrated to Harlem during this time period. Because the south was not economically advantageous for blacks, many settled into northern territories where opportunities were vast. Harlem became home for nearly 175,000 blacks- the largest concentration of blacks worldwide. It is here, where The New Negro Movement evolved.

Three Plays for a Negro Theatre was the first play to showcase an entire black cast. Many believe this was the first stage of the New Negro Movement. Written by white playwright Frederick Ridgley Torrence, this play captured the strength and raw emotion portrayed by Negro actors. Because of recent cultural and social changes, freedom of expression for blacks was imperative. Their emotions were very real and symbolized their struggle. Many artist of The Harlem Renaissance movement were children and grandchildren of former slaves. Although slavery had legally ended, racism continued to be dominant in the south and others parts of the country. By way of literary commentary black artist spoke out for change. They all sought a better way of life and racial independence. James Weldon Johnson reviewed Three Plays for a Negro Theatre as "the most important single event in the entire history of the negro in American history."

The Harlem Renaissance era continues to inspire because of the courageousness each artist portrayed. Bear in mind, this era occurred during a time of extreme challenge. Writers and creative artist alike were compelled to express themselves despite potential risk. Each of them, committed to raising awareness of the cultural issues present in hopes of creating a better tomorrow. It is because of their will, we have change.

Generally speaking, getting people to read on purpose is a challenge. Outside of the mandatory college books, most adults do not actively engage in reading. According to Jenkins Group INC, 70% of adults have not visited a bookstore for the last 5 years and 42% of college graduates never read after college. Yet, the illiteracy rate in the United States of America is astounding. Only 1 in 7 adults are literate and Detroit has a 47% illiteracy rate. Reading is important because words in print create energy! Fueling the need for literature to live on! The <u>I Have a Dream</u> speech by Martin Luther King Jr. continues to energize many because of the power of his words! Writing and reading is the core of human creativity. It is the words spoken to us, lyrics heard in songs, and most importantly the words we read in books that gives birth to change. This book was created for the purpose of providing inspiration to others. It is my sincerest hope that the words you will read in this book, will not only inspire…but also will positively change your life!

SECTION I
TRUTH

*"Faith and prayer are the vitamins of the soul.
Many cannot live in health without them"*

Mahalia Jackson ~ Legendary Gospel Singer

The SEED

Religion is how man defines God, but faith is a personal choice. Faith requires making a private heartfelt decision about who God is and what role he plays in your life. For some, God is omniscience- all knowing. To others, God's power is unlimited omnipotence. Many call HIM omnipresent or omnibenevolent- presents to all; perfect everywhere.

God means many things to many people. Aside from our chosen paths of faith, through prayer we find understanding, clarity and direction. Great plans are achieved when prayer becomes an active part of our daily lives. Life void of spirituality is livable but prayer is needed to rejuvenate our spirits. Through prayer, we are able communicate with our supernatural source and become sustained.

Today's Affirmative:
Prayer sustains me.

*"Bad human communication
leaves less room to grow."*

*Rowan D. Williams ~
Anglican Bishop, Poet and Theologian*

Great Communication

Historically there have been various forms of communication before human speech was perfected. Cave paintings are the oldest method of communication dating back to approximately 30,000 B.C. Located in southern France, The Chauvet Pont-d'Arc Cave is a prehistoric rock art site, home to various ancient animal art sketches. These sketches are believed to have been used for communicating messages to cave inhabitants.

Throughout history, articulation has always been important. Insufficient communication creates barriers and hides truth. Being honest and thorough restores relationships, corrects problems, and reveals ideas. Many of our problems would be solved if only we made a serious effort to communicate with one another effectively.

Today's Affirmative:
I will consider my speech and conduct wisely.

For the Kingdom of God
is not a matter of talk but of power

1 Corinthians 4:20 NIV

Godly Power

The supernatural power that our lives require does not live on paper. Instead, God's power becomes alive when we apply it to our lives! Actors prepare for scripts, to enable their words to be believable. Recall the infamous "You can't handle the truth" line by Jack Nicholson in A Few Good Men? I imagine he practiced these words and his expressions repeatedly before he was able to deliver these lines with perfection.

We are not actors however we are active participants in this play called life. Our action may not attract national attention but our performance does matter. Just as Rob Reiner expected his cast to remember the script and deliver it with greatness, so does our heavenly director. Divine power is released when words become actions!

Today's Affirmative:
God's power is inside of me.

"My idea of good company of clever well informed people who have a great deal of conversation; that is what I call good company."

Jane Austen ~ English Novelist

Good Company

All we can do is try to lead our lives by example, and hope our actions inspire others positively. Arguing, backbiting, and gossip are all avoidable and unnecessary energy. The company we choose to keep is a direct reflection on us and has an impact on the goals we aim for.

Deciding to overcome an addiction will mean sacrificing dependent friendships. Committing to a life of prosperity means no more unwise spending. Becoming a positive person means giving up negative relationships. Whatever our goal, we should always be equipped with the tools and company needed to reach our accomplishments. Behind every successful person is a positive, successful team.

Today's Affirmative:
I must prepare for success.

*"Don't leave inferences to be drawn
when evidence can be presented."*

Richard Wright ~ Harlem Renaissance Contributor

Ill Informed

It is very dangerous to accept the feelings of others as truth because perception is personal. Our opinions change and our emotions can fluctuate at any given moment for any reason. What we "feel" and what "really is" can be confusing.

Misinformation almost always creates confusion. This confusion causes division, and division eliminates unity. With love and peace we find truth.

Today's Affirmative:
I cannot lead with only emotion.

A good man brings good things out of the good stored up in his heart, and an evil man brings evil things out of the evil stored up in his heart. For the mouth speaks what the heart is full of.

Luke 6:45 NIV

Courage

We are all guilty of saying something inappropriate at one time or another. Without thought we show error because we are human. Although laughter can ofen ease a tense situation it does not negate our poor choice of words. Being conscience of our words shows humility and wisdom. If we should offend anyone in our behavior, we should always do what is honorable and offer an apology. Attempting to conceal our mistakes through humor is disingenuous and unhelpful.

Though needed and appreciated, apologies are difficult. No matter how obvious the fault, the words "I'm sorry" seem to always be difficult to say. The Vatican apologized for their failure to respond to the Nazi regime in an attempt to foster healing on past wounds. In February of 2011, Archbishop Gregory Aymond referred to racism as "sinful", as he offered an apology on behalf of The New Orleans Church for participating in slavery. And yet still today, there continues to a debate on an appropriate remedy for enslavement of black people. Admitting mistakes take courage.

Today's Affirmative:
I have the heart of a champion, not a coward.

"Education is that whole system of human training within and without the school house, which molds and develops men."

W.E.B. Du Bois ~ Harlem Renaissance Contributor

Lesson Learned

There are tremendous amounts of emphasis placed on institutionalized education. Education enriches our being and helps contribute to the social progression of society. It is widely believed, that education produces a higher quality of life. On the other hand, a formal education (or lack thereof), does not guarantee prosperous living.

The bible says:

We can rejoice, too, when we run into problems and trials, for we know that they help us develop endurance. And endurance develops strength of character, and character strengthens our confident hope of salvation. And this hope will not lead to disappointment. For we know how dearly God loves us, because he has given us the Holy Spirit to fill our hearts with his love. Romans 5:3-5

Society has groomed many to believe that formal education is the only key to success. It is assumed that those who lack higher education cannot valuably contribute nor become astute leaders in society. Despite popular notions, experience remains one of life's best teachers. Through our struggles, mistakes and disappointments, comprehension is gained. Somehow the lessons of life guide us, as we recall upon the wisdom of experience. Formal education is important, but we must also remember there are lessons to be learned with every reality.

Today's Affirmative:
Every experience is a lesson.

For my thoughts are not your thoughts. Neither your ways my ways saith the Lord. For as the heavens are higher than the earth, so are my ways higher than your ways, and my thoughts than your thoughts.

Isaiah 55: 8-9 KJV

Trusting the Source

Belief in God and trusting God are not the same things. Trust requires action. It requires that we remain unshakable during the most difficult of circumstances. Trust requires total faith even when we do not understand. Belief is merely an idea.

My walk with the Lord has certainly not been without blemish. At times I was focused and unmoved whereas equally there have been times when my faith was not assured. Through tragedies and disappointments every believer has days of questionable faith.

Perhaps you are facing difficulties in your life. Maybe there are struggles you are facing that you cannot understand. Contrary to popular belief, all of us have days like these. What is most important is knowing who holds tomorrow and whom you can trust with your future. Where is your confidence? Is it in your job? Your spouse? Your family? Any of these can change without warning. God never promised that everyday would be filled with happiness, but we can rest knowing he is in control even when we do not understand.

Today's Affirmative:
Be still and know.

"I am personally convinced that one person can be a change catalyst, a "transformer" in any situation, any organization. Such an individual is yeast that can leaven an entire loaf. It requires vision, initiative, patience, respect, persistence, courage, and faith to be a transforming leader."

Stephen R. Covey ~ Author

Makings of a Leader

What makes a quality leader? Many are misguided on the principals of good leadership. Status, education, and wealth can all contribute to the success of leadership, however none of these qualities truly defines a leader. Success, much like leadership, is based on your ability to overcome and impact the lives around you. Sure, we can all thrive in a stress free environment, but what challenge is found in this? Good leaders set the standard by making a difference. Effective leadership promotes change and makes others become better.

Today's Affirmative:
Leaders do not self-serve.

Moreover if your brother sins against you, go and tell him his fault between you and him alone.
If he hears you, you have gained your brother

Matthew 18:15 NKJV

Real Talk

Take your problems to the source.

No two persons think alike. When we fail to communicate our concerns with one another we miss an opportunity for resolution. In fact, involving other people in our matters of difference can make things worse. The best way to resolve conflict is by confronting issues head-on with respect. Make a conscious effort to listen, accept constructive criticism, and avoid being defensive. We can solve many of our problems if we dump the middle man and address our concerns directly.

Today's Affirmative:
Gossip creates more problems than it solves.

"If a man is not faithful to his own individuality he cannot be loyal to anything."

Claude McKay ~ Harlem Renaissance Contributor

Looking in the Mirror

Reality television, and celebrity websites highlight not only the lives of the rich and famous, but even average and sometimes dysfunctional people command our attention. For some reason the lives of others always appear more interesting than our own.

While influence can be good, not everything we see, hear or read is positive. Self-awareness is something that is missing in our youth as many of them are imitating the wrong behaviors they see. Every youth needs positive, accessible tangible role models to look towards and become inspired by.

Today's Affirmative:
It starts with me.

"We are mere journeymen planting seeds for someone else to harvest."

Wallace Thurman ~ Harlem Renaissance Contributor

First Fruits

As we are blessed it is our responsibility to pass those gifts onto someone else. We should all aspire to make life better for everyone by passing our knowledge onto others. Many undervalue their contributions by neglecting to help, but favor comes with investment.

Consider your life. Everything about your life has been influenced by someone else. Your moral values, integrity, religious beliefs, all were shaped and molded by a keeper of the faith. We are charged to pass on what we were given, to help someone else in need.

Today's Affirmative:
Reaping comes after the harvest.

SECTION II
TRAGEDY

"When people care for you and cry for you, they can straighten out your soul."

Langston Hughes ~Harlem Renaissance Contributor

Gift of Charity

2009 was considered a down year for charitable contributions in the United States. Only $303.75 billion dollars were accumulated from private citizens, corporations and foundations. Despite this enormous amount, this is a 3.2 percent decline from the previous year. These statistics suggest, despite economic challenges people remain committed to give. There is something humanizing about helping those in need. This feeling of comfort energizes our spirit and replenishes our soul.

Although compassion can be demonstrated through financial gifts, money does not meet every need. The needs of many extend beyond debt; as some hope for peace. The emotional sacrifices we make on behalf of one another are priceless. Mourning on behalf of a friend is charitable. An organ donor submits a tremendous gift when helping to save a life. Healing is found when attention is shown to the disabled, elderly, and children. Compassion is love in its immeasurable form.

Today's Affirmative:
I will put the needs of others ahead of my own today.

*"When there is pain there are no words.
All pain is the same."*

Toni Morrison ~
Nobel Prize and Pulitzer Prize winning novelist

Pain Pushes Our Passion

Sometimes we have to make the stars align by strategically positioning ourselves for our blessings. Good things come to those who wait. Great things come to those who wait in preparation. We have to prepare for greatness! Eliminate the meager, non-fruitful matters by focusing on greatness. Opportunity is present in every situation.

Today's Affirmative:
P.U.S.H.

"So in the dark we hide the heart that bleeds, and wait, and tend our agonizing seeds."

Countee Cullen ~ Harlem Renaissance Contributor

Love Heals

Hurt is the consequence of physical, spiritual, emotional or mental injury and our hearts heal and hold all of these. When we ignore the pain, we avoid reliving the agony but these grievances are cancerous and the longer we omit treatment, the more hazardous they grow. Love is the only cure for everything.

Today's Affirmative:
Love heals. This includes learning to love myself.

"If a man calls me nigger, it's his fault the first time, but mine if he has the opportunity to do it again."

Nella Larsen ~ Harlem Renaissance Contributor

Stand

Any language used with the intent to offend is intolerable and we should not be afraid to speak out against it. The word "nigger" is the most detestable word in American history. Not only is this term derogatory to persons of African descent, usage of this phrase stirs unpleasant memories of slavery and the mistreatment of persons of color.

There are many variants of this term as it was originally spelled as "neigers" dating back to 1568, when it first appeared in Thomas Hackett and Andre' Thevet 's novel, A New Found Worlde. The modern term "nigger" later appeared during the 1800's and unfortunately continues to be used in speech, literature, urban rap music, and even in our private conversations to date.

Despite its' commonality, the utterance of this word is reprehensible and should never be regarded as acceptable or excused as a term of endearment. It will always be the ugliest language in American History and is unacceptable for any person who chooses to use it.

Today's Affirmative:
Free speech is no longer free, when we use expressions of hate.

"You may encounter many defeats, but you must not be defeated. In fact, it may be necessary to encounter the defeats, so you can know who you are, what you can rise from, how you can still come out of it."

Maya Angelou ~ Famous Poet

Keep Rising to the Top

True strength comes from weakness. If you do not first know what it is like to feel embattled how can you learn how to be strong? It is a myth that the successes of life comes from mistake free living. In fact, a life without faults does not exist.

My personal struggles are the true motivation behind this book. There were many times in life when I felt defeated and wanted to give up. Many days I felt hopeless and useless. I know what it is like to be hungry and to go without many of life's necessity's including shelter, a job, income and even friends. This is how I learned sometimes it is necessary to lose in order to gain.

Today's Affirmative:
A goal delayed is not a goal denied.

"I must lose myself in action, lest I wither in despair."

Alfred Lord Tennyson~ English Poet

Trouble Don't Last Always

Trouble is so easy to get into, yet three times as hard to overcome. Especially when the trouble we face is a result of our own doing. Wallowing in defeat is simply not an option during these times, because a worry wart will never produce any clear results.

We have all had times of despair, regret, and sorrow in our lives. It is during these difficulties, when we are likely to make poor choices that will further our anxieties. No matter how steep the valley, you can still make it to the top by beginning with the first step.

Today Affirmative:
My past transgressions will not dictate my future.

"It was books that taught me that the things that tormented me most were the very things that connected me with all the people who were alive or who ever had been alive."

James A. Baldwin ~ Harlem Renaissance Contributor

Powerless

The reason why I write is simple: To help promote literacy. Too many of us cannot read or write and fail to engage. This is also the top reason why many of us are powerless. In order to incite change, one must be informed. In order to become informed one must READ. Illiteracy is a real epidemic in our communities. This is unacceptable and cannot continue.

Without knowledge we do not have the power to move forward. There are many educational materials found on television the World Wide Web, and other media sources. But if technology were to ever fail, history is lost without books. If we fail to prepare our future (children) with the necessary skill set of reading, how can they compete? We do ourselves a disservice when we do not take literacy seriously and fail to pass these habits onto our children. It should be every one's educational, moral and ethical responsibility to READ. READ to your children. Encourage your students to READ. Take interest in a book, or a blog that is uplifting and resourceful. Share this information with your friends and inspire them to develop an active interest in reading.

Today's Affirmative:
I am powerless without information.

SECTION III
TRIUMPH

"*You are young, gifted and black. We must begin to tell our young there's a world waiting for you, yours is the quest that is just begun.*"

James Weldon Johnson ~
Harlem Renaissance Contributor

Destined to Be Great

To be considered a master at any game is superb. A chess master is considered a player of extreme skill. As master, you are expected to easily win against any novice player. The title of "chess master" is held by 47,000 people and of these only 85 are African American. These young men are of rare accomplishment and have reached this leadership status before the age of 13. "Masters don't happen every day, and African-American masters who are 12 never happen," said Maurice Ashley, 45, the only African-American to earn the top title of grandmaster.

Chess has always interested me because it is a game of intense concentration and skill. Many adults who regularly engage fail to reach an elite status and truthfully still struggle to task the game. I have never been any good at chess, because I fail to demonstrate the discipline and study this game requires. It is an amazing achievement that young men were able to reach this caliber early on in life. Their success shows no goal is too large to accomplish. The only driving force between greatness and mediocrity is you!

Today's Affirmative:
I am destined to be great!

"He who is not courageous to take risks will accomplish nothing in life"

Muhammad Ali ~
Legendary Boxer

The Little Engine that Could

Doing things the easy way is effortless. Anyone can cruise through life doing the bare minimum. But it will be those persons who take that leap of faith that will land in the thick of success. Every historic accomplishment was not without chance. Pioneers believed in their causes, their dreams, and expectations wholeheartedly. They were not fearful of the unknown.

Today's Affirmative:
You never know until you try.

"There is no secret to success except hard work and getting something indefinable..."

Countee Cullen ~ Harlem Renaissance Contributor

Victorious

Success is dependent upon our earnest efforts. It is equally important to not only set goals but to actively engage our visions by developing a plan for success. Understanding your purpose is key. The leaders of our past have provided a foundation for us to build upon by displaying courage to task. We learned from their efforts that a willingness to fight is an essential part of victory. None can afford to sit idly and wait for dreams to become reality.

Today's Affirmative:
Action is the gas that drives the car.

"No person is your friend who demands your silence or denies your right to grow."

Alice Walker – Author

Friend or Foe

The word "friend" is used fairly loosely these days. People we encounter at work, school, or in passing are incorrectly labeled as "friend", even though we know very little about that person. What is more humorous is they likely know even less about us. Why then do we use the term "friend" so casually? Commonly we confuse a kind word, gesture or conversation as friend instead of friendly. Every smiling face does not have your best interest. In some instances, even a helping hand does not ascertain friendship. A confidant is someone you can trust wholeheartedly without question. Confidants, keep your secrets, share in your pain and celebrate your progress. Their loyalty cannot be measured because their support is endless. Their expressions of love are meaningful. A true friend's worth is priceless!

Today's Affirmative:
I will learn my friends by the fruit they bear.

"Talk about it only enough to do it
Dream about it only enough to feel it
Think about it only enough to understand it
Contemplate it only enough to be it."

Jean Toomer ~ Harlem Renaissance Contributor

No Boundaries

We create the walls by which we are bound. It is our lack of desire to do something different; lack of dare of what might become, that stops us from excelling to the heights of life. Often people avoid aiming for the top because of fear; however, if we never take any risk there can never be any reward. Things do not happen unless we make them happen. Choose to let go of whatever is holding you back from experiencing the best that life has to offer.

Today's Affirmative:
There is no limit to what I can do.

"Each person must live their life as a model for others."

Rosa Parks ~ Civil Rights Activist

Life, Camera, Action

While the opinions of others should never be our primary focus, reputation is important because our behaviors reveal much about who we really are. The times in which we live, call for all of us to step up, lead, and inspire! Without notice, onlookers are watching and deciphering our every move. Some will use our lives as examples by learning from our truths and triumphs. Others are inspired by how we handle adversity and rise above the challenge. We can never be sure who is observing us therefore we must always be ready to give an account for our conduct.

Rosa Parks is an excellent example of how personal conduct can make a difference. Quietly, Rosa Parks worked behind the scenes at the local NAACP assisting with voter registration and leading the youth. It was her refusal to give up her seat on the bus that commanded the attention of an entire nation. Her courage inspired the official start of the Montgomery Movement, which eventually led to end of legal segregation.

Today's Affirmative:
My life can make a difference!

"Don't let nobody tell you what you can't do"

Dewey Bozella ~ Exonerated Boxer

Believe in You

What is holding you back from pursuing your dreams?
Fear of failure or fear of yourself? The number one
roadblock to achieving the impossible is: YOU! Many
desire the reward, yet few are willing to contribute
what is required. Sheer determination brings life to
ideas and makes our dreams become a reality.

Born in 1959, Dewey Bozellla is an amazing testament
of courage. Improperly incarcerated for 26 years,
Dewey was released in 2009 and exonerated of any
crime. Prior to his murder sentence in 1983, Dewey
spent much of his life in survival mode. Persuaded to
overcome all odds, Dewey developed into a young
quality street fighter who spent time training in
Brooklyn New York. His goal was to find success
through his tragedies. During his sentence at Sing Sing
Correctional Facility, Dewey became a light
heavyweight boxing champion. His lifelong goal of
winning a professional fight was achieved on October
15, 2011.

Many lose faith in their abilities based on the opinions
of others. Some stop short of reaching for the stars
simply because someone said it was impossible. Don't
allow the thoughts of others to determine your legacy.
Become empowered by your spirit and keep striving
for the top.

Today's Affirmative:
I can choose to daydream or dream catch.

"Being underestimated is sometimes a strategy"

Reverend Al Sharpton~
Political and Civil Rights Activist

Underestimated

In 2010, the New Orleans Saints football team was crowned Super Bowl XLIV Champions. Most viewed this victory as a major success for New Orleans because of the devastation of Hurricane Katrina in 2005. The New Orleans Saints achievement brought tremendous uplifting to an already challenged city.

Their win is certainly inspirational, but what is even more motivating is how the team was able to work together to accomplish this goal. Many of the players on the 2009 roster were considered has-beens. Several of them had been unsigned or traded by other highly rated NFL teams. They were viewed as athletes who could no longer deliver the goods. They were underestimated not only in ability; but, also in what they would be able to accomplish. Prior to 2009, very few believed in the city or the football team.

Very often we discredit the ability of others and ourselves based on what we see. We conclude the ending of one's story without giving weight to what is truly important. Sometimes, the rank and file of life is not accurate. It is character, heart, and determination that truly fuels your success.

Today's Affirmative:
God sees the best in us.

"Everyone thinks of changing the world,
but no one thinks of changing himself"

Leo Tolstoy ~ Russian Writer

Change the World

There is something about newness everyone appreciates. Very often, it is the quest of new things that drive us to do better. We tend to work harder when there is a goal to reach and extreme goals require making extreme changes. While it is less risky to live a life of routine, going with the flow is common. Going against the grain sets us apart and gets different results. Do not drift through life comfortably. Challenge yourself to become better in every area. Through our thoughts, mannerisms, and deeds we are able to create a brighter today. Be willing to make any necessary changes, if progress is what you truly desire.

Today's Affirmative:
Change is good.

SECTION IV
HARLEM RENAISSANCE CONTRIBUTORS

ARNA WENDELL BONTEMPS

1902-1973

Encouraged to deny his racial heritage by his forbearer, Arna Wendell Bontemps was a family man, dedicated to supporting his family. As a husband and father to six children, Arna accepted a teaching position in 1924 at the Harlem Academy in New York City, which led to his involvement with the Harlem Renaissance movement. Best known for his novel, <u>God Sends Sunday</u>, Bontemps earned the Jane Adams Books award for his critically acclaimed work <u>The Story of the Negro</u>. He also co-wrote the 1946 stage play <u>St. Louis Woman </u>with Countee Cullen. Recently, his birthplace in Alexandria Louisiana was converted to the Bontemps African American Museum in his honor.

COUNTEE CULLEN

1903-1946

A leader in the Harlem Renaissance movement, Countee Cullen was an admirable award-winning poet and composer, who also engaged in teaching English, French and creative writing. Color, his first collection of poetry, was published in 1926, a year after graduating from New York University. Cullen was considered modest, remaining mostly private about the details of his life. His poetic and literary achievements continue to define him as one of the more successful Harlem Renaissance figures, as he is the recipient of the most literary awards to any black writer during the 1920s.

W.E.B. Du Bois
1868-1963

Famous for beginning the Harlem Renaissance
movement, W.E.B. Du Bois is remembered for his
historic civic and literary service within the African
American community. In 1905, Du Bois co-founded the
Niagra Movement with William M. Trotter, a
determined effort in the quest of racial equality and
civil rights for blacks. W.E.B. Du Bois sought for blacks
to be recognized as people of color, rather than
regarded as negroes. He was strongly opposed to the
Atlanta Compromise; a deal crafted by Booker T.
Washington that aimed to relinquish equal and fair
treatment of blacks, in exchange for jobs, education and
legal due process. As illustrated in <u>The Souls of Black
Folk,</u> DuBois was passionate about advancing
opportunities for blacks and his lives works are
dedicated to this purpose.

Jesse Redmond Fauset
1882-1961

One of the lesser contributors in the Harlem Renaissance movement, Jesse worked relentlessly behind the scenes providing editing services for the more prominent New Negro Movement artist. A writer herself, Fauset's novel Plum Bun has been referred to academically and she is remembered for her contributions and service.

Rudolph Fisher
1897-1934

Together with Hughes, Cullen, Hurston and DuBois, Rudolph Fisher was the core of the Harlem Renaissance movement. He contributed to this literary era with both writings and music and was a fervent chronicler of social history. Much of his writings aimed to ease racial tensions during these times. Fisher is a Howard University medical school graduate and former superintendent of the first black owned international hospital in Harlem.

Nella Larsen
1891-1964

Although she only published a few literary works,
Nella Larsen is remembered for her writing
contributions during the Harlem Renaissance era.   Her
novels were critically acclaimed, as they often focused
on the lives and treatment of mixed raced females.
Larsen worked at Tuskegee Institute as head nurse of
both the hospital and training schools.   After being
accused of plagiarism n 1930 , and undergoing an
emotional divorce, Nella would never write literature
again after 1933.

Alain LeRoy Locke
1885-1954

Hailed as the "Father of the Harlem Renaissance",
Alain LeRoy Locke was a strong motivating figure
behind the success of the Harlem Renaissance
movement. He encouraged all blacks during this era,
to refer back to Africa as an inspirational guide. Locke
was self-assured and possessed a wealth of political
awareness. He believed that "ideas flourish through
action", and he pushed this message to all he mentored,
including Zora Neale Hurston.   Locke is certainly
remembered for his efforts nationwide, as several
schools have been named in his honor in parts of
Indiana, Los Angeles, Philadelphia and Chicago.

Herbert Harrison
1883-1927

Strong, astute, compassionate and spirited are all
accurate attributes used to describe Hubert Harrison.
Harrison was a multilingual gifted intellectual, well
versed in black history and concerned about the
welfare and treatment of his people. A Virgin Island
native, Hubert was shocked by the treatment of blacks
in the United States. His vast knowledge was used to
promote self-awareness in people of color. He was the
first black book reviewer, and founded the first
newspaper of the New negro Movement era, <u>The Voice</u>.
He also chaired the Negro American Liberty Congress,
which was a united movement against segregation in
the United States.

Langston Mercer Hughes
1902-1967

Langston James Mercer Hughes is a legendary
innovator of jazz poetry because he was able to infuse
the soul of jazz music into his poetic literary works.
The Negro Speaks of Rivers became his signature
poem and was first published in W.E.B. Du Bois' The
Crisis. The difference of opinions in career paths
would contribute to the poor relationship Hughes had
with his father. His father agreed to support him
financially if he pursued an engineering career, but
Langston was passionate about pursuing literature. He
is credited for his instrumental literary contributions,
particularly during the Harlem Renaissance era.

James Weldon Johnson
1871-1938

Blessed with strong, solid roots, James Weldon Johnson is known for his NAACP leadership and civil rights activism. He is the son of Louise Dillet, the first black female teacher at Edwin M. Stanton located in Florida. James brother John Rosamond is the famous composer of the Negro National Anthem- Life Every Voice and Sing. James Weldon Johnson is remembered for his trusted literary and civil contribution.

Claudius McKay
1889-1948

Racism largely inspired Claude McKay's poetry. A
well-traveled Jamaican native, McKay was shocked by
the levels of racism that existed in the United States and
the poor treatment of blacks. His poetry writings
would help to set the tone for the New Negro
Movement. In 1928, he became the Harmon Gold
winner for his bestselling novel, <u>Home to Harlem</u>. A
collection of his poetry is located in the James Weldon
Johnson collection at Yale University.

George Schuyler
1895-1977

While many have debated George Schuyler's racial
loyalty, no one can doubt his literary gifts. Schuyler
has an accomplished literary resume including
positions as an assistant editor of <u>The Messenger</u>,
Columnist of <u>Shafts and Darts</u>, New York
correspondent for the Pittsburg Courier, as well as
various weekly commentaries on race relations and
other social issues. <u>The Negro Art Hokum</u> is one of his
most controversial pieces in addition to his scientific
novel <u>Black No More</u>, which toys with the idea of
turning black folks white. Schuyler is of mixed racial
heritage.

Carl Van Vechten
1880-1964

Although the Harlem Renaissance was dominated by
African American literary figures, its impact carried a
much broader scope. As a white photographer and
writer, Carl Van Vechten was heavily interested in
black authors and artist who were major Harlem
Renaissance figures. Born in Iowa, Van Wechten
became a graduate of the University of Chicago. Chi
Town is where he developed his interest of the arts,
while exploring music and literature. In 1906 Van
Wechten relocated to the New York area, where he
became assistant musical director at the New York
Times. He later went on to become the first American
critic of modern dance. Carl Van Vechten spent his
later years in life involved in photography and writing.
His involvement in the Harlem Renaissance movement
continues to be an instrumental part of history.

SECTION V
ABOUT THE AUTHOR

About the Author

As thriving entrepreneur and owner of RDW Creations, Rosey Denise White has long maintained a love for writing. From adolescents through adulthood, Rosey has always held a passion for literature. She enjoys English and has a special interest in Greek literature. Inspiring others through thought provoking materials is her literary aspiration. She believes readers of all backgrounds can connect to the real-life approach that her literature often produces. Her non-traditional realistic style has garnered the attention of community leaders, business professionals and novice readers alike.

A Cass Technical Alum, Rosey hails from Detroit, Michigan with roots extending to the southern parts of the country. She is also the award winner of the Floyd M. Washington Jr. essay contest, co-sponsored by the Detroit NAACP and Ford Motor Company.

As a member of the Motown Writers Network, Rosey works with other local authors who enjoy the written word, and strive to strengthen Michigan's literary community. In her spare time, she enjoys reading, writing and listening to music. She is an avid sports fan and also enjoys leisurely travels.

Rosey believes writing is her divine gift. She aspires to influence current and future generations through her current and future literary works.

REFERENCES

Alain Leroy Locke Biography Howard University
   Libraries. Retrieved December 2011,
   http://foundrs.howard.edu/Locke.htm

African American Quotes Retrieved December 2011
   http://africanamericanquotes.org/james-weldon-
   johnson.html

Biblegateway Retrieve October 2011 http:
   biblegatewway.com/passage/?search=1%20Corint
   hians%2047version=NIV

Biblegateway Retrieved October 2011,
   http://biblegateway.com/passage/?search-
   Luke5206:45&version=NIV

Biblegateway Retrieved October 2011,
   http://biblegateway.com/passage/?search-
   isaiah%2055:8-9&version=KJV

Black Boy Reading Woman Retrieved, October 2010
   http://readingwoman.com/autobiography.html#bl
   ackboy

Carl Van Vechten Biography The Library of Congress

Retrieved November 2011
http://memory.loc.gov/ammeem/collections/v anvechten/vvbio.html

Dave Wilton Retrieved December 2006 Word Orgins
http://wordorgins.org/index.php/site/comments /nigger/

DuBois, William Edward Bughardt, Retrieved September 2011,
http://pabook.libraries.psu.edu/palitmap/bios/Bu Bois_wEB.html

Ethel Waters Retrieved October 2011,
http://redhotjazz.com/waters.html

Fauset, Jessie Redmon, Retrieved October 2011
http://pabook.libraries.psu.edu/palitmap/bios.fau set_Jesse_Redmon.html

George S. Schuyler Goodreads Retrieved August 2010,
http://goodreads.com/author.show/210306.Georg e_S_Schuyler

Jane Austen Quotes Brainy Quote
Retrieved June 2010
http://brainyquote.com/quotes/authors/j/jane_a usten.html

Langston Hughes Quotes Brainy Quote
Retrieved June 2010
http://brainyquote.com/quotes/authors/l/langsto n_hughes.html.

Modern American Poetry Retrieved November 2001,
http://english.illinois.edu/Maps/poets/m_r/mckay.h
tm

Biblegateway Retrieve October 2011 http:
biblegatewway.com/passage/?search=1%20Corint
hians%2047version=NIV

Rosa Parks Biography Academy of Achievement
Retrieved November 2011,
http://achievement.org/autodoc/page/par0bio-1

The Academy of American Poets
Retrieved October 2010,
http://poets.org/poet.php/prmPID/128

The Center on Philanthropy at Indiana University
Retrieved October 2010,
http://philanthropy.iupui.edu/news/2010/pr-
GUSA2010.aspx

The Voice of Early 20th Century Harlem Radicalism
Retrieved September 2011,
http://blackpast.org/?=perspectives/hubert-
harrison-voice-early-20th-century-harlem-
radicalism.

http://brainyquote.com/quotes/authors/j/jane_a
usten.html.

Wallace Thurman Quotes Brainy Quote
Retrieved October 2010
http://brainyquote.com/quotes/authors/w/walla
ce_thurman_.html.

www.ingramcontent.com/pod-product-compliance
Lightning Source LLC
Chambersburg PA
CBHW060952040426
42445CB00011B/1117